Soccer

Bernie Blackall

Heinemann Library
Des Plaines, Illinois

03 02 01 00 99
10 9 8 7 6 5 4 3 2 1

Series cover and text design by Karen Young
Cover by Smarty-pants Design
Paged by Jo Pritchard
Edited by Jane Pearson
Illustrations by Vasja Koman
Picture research by Lara Artis and Kirsty Grant
Production by Cindy Smith
Film separations by Type Scan, Adelaide
Printed in Hong Kong by Wing King Tong

Library of Congress Cataloging-in-Publication Data

Blackall, Bernie, 1956-
     Soccer / Bernie Blackall.
          p.   cm. -- (Top sport)
     Includes bibliographical references and index.
     Summary: Introduces the history, skills, rules, equipment, events,
and highlights of soccer.
     ISBN 1-57572-840-0 (library binding)
     1. Soccer -- Juvenile literature. 2. Soccer--Australia--Juvenile
literature. [1. Soccer.] I. Title. II. Series: Blackall,
Bernie, 1956- Top sport.
     GV943.25.B516   1999
     796.334--dc21
                                                     98-45917
                                                         CIP
                                                          AC

Acknowledgments
The author and publisher are grateful to the following for permission to
reproduce copyright material:
Bernie Blackall, p. 15; Coo-ee Historical Picture Library, p. 8; Henri Szwarc,
p. 24; Joe Mann, p. 5; Joe Sabljak, p. 22; Sport/The Library, pp. 9, 13;
Sue and Wies Fajzullin Photography, pp. 4, 5, 10, 11, 16, 18, 19, 21, 25;
Liles Photography, pp. 20, 23, 26; DUOMO/Chris Cole, p 7;
SportsChrome USA/Rob Tringali Jr, p. 6.

Every effort has been made to contact copyright holders of any material
reproduced in this book. Any omissions will be rectified in subsequent
printings if notice is given to the publisher.

Some words are shown in bold, **like this.** You can
find out what they mean by looking in the glossary.

Special thanks to Larry McCorkle, United States Soccer
Federation "A" Licensed Coach and member of the Florida
Coaches' Hall of Fame.

Contents

About Soccer

Soccer is a team sport in which two teams of 11 players compete. Each team tries to score goals by kicking or heading the ball into their opponent's goal. They also must defend their goal when their opponents have possession of the ball. The 10 field players may play the ball with their feet, head, or body, but never with their arms or hands. The eleventh player is the **goalkeeper**. He or she is the only player allowed to handle the ball, but only from within a certain area in front of the goal.

A senior soccer match consists of two 45-minute halves. A junior match consists of two 20- or 25-minute halves.

World's most popular sport

Soccer is the world's most popular sport. It has 130 million male and female players throughout the world. It is played in more than 180 countries. The 1994 World Cup soccer tournament was the most-watched television sporting event of all time. It even exceeded the popularity of the Atlanta Olympics of 1996.

Traditionally, soccer has been a game for male players, but recently it has become popular with female players, too. This trend is certain to grow as women's soccer takes its place in the Olympic Games in Sydney, Australia, for the second time in the year 2000.

U.S. Highlights

Cobi Jones

Until the arrival of Pelé, the Brazilian superstar, to the New York Cosmos in 1975, it was doubtful whether soccer could kick its way into the hearts of American sports fans. Afterall, the homegrown sports of baseball, basketball, and American football left little passion for an "imported" sport like soccer.

Against all odds, from the 1970s on, soccer has become the fastest growing team sport in the United States.

The MLS in The USA

Things have changed. Most importantly, the U.S. hosted the World Cup in 1994. The games were played here with the promise that a professional league would be formed in the U.S.

Mia Hamm

Mia Hamm, shown here during the 1996 Olympics, will lead the U.S. Women's team in the 1999 Women's World Cup, which is being held in the U.S.

In 1996, MLS became the first successful Division 1 Soccer League in the United States since 1984. It is the only U.S. league to be sanctioned by both the USSF (United States Soccer Federation) and FIFA (Federation Internationale de Football Association.) In its first season, an average of 17,286 fans attended the games.

In 1998, Miami and Chicago joined the league. In its first season, the Chicago Fire won the MLS Cup at the Rose Bowl Stadium in Pasadena, CA. The Fire beat two-time champions D.C. United. Superstar, Peter Nowak won a championship for the first time in his career.

Other American favorites in the MLS include Tony Meola, Eddie Pope, Cobi Jones, Brian McBride, Alexi Lalas, John Harkes, and Marcelo Balboa. Today, 12 teams compete in the conference. MLS plans to add four more teams to the league by 2002.

Women's Soccer

1996 was a stellar year for U.S. soccer. The Women's National Team came home from the Olympic Games in Atlanta, GA with the gold. Mia Hamm and her teammates were in the spotlight and now have a huge number of devoted fans. Mia Hamm is the first athlete to have been named U.S. Soccer's Female Athlete of the Year three years in a row. Previous titleholders include Kristine Lilly, Carin Gabarra, and Michelle Akers.

History of Soccer

The exact origins of modern soccer are unknown, but similar games have been played for centuries. The ancient Greeks played a soccer-like game called *episkyros*, in which a large ball was moved by any means possible to a goal line. Refined and improved by the Romans, the game *harpastum* limited ball movement to kicking and hitting with the hands.

Football

Later, the game was called "football" because only the feet could touch the ball. The Romans took the game to England, where it became very popular. But several English Kings banned football because it interfered with military training and because of its roughness and high rate of serious injury.

a soccer match in 1914

In 1966, England won the World Cup, which is the greatest achievement in soccer.

Football became an attraction for many fairs and festivals. Sometimes games were played with 500 people on each team. In 1581, Queen Elizabeth I banned football in London, England, because of damage caused to shops and property when people played in the streets.

Rules

The game was played in many English schools in the early 1800s, but it had no formal rules. Later two sets of rules developed. At one school, Rugby, a set of rules was made to include handling and running with the ball. The game of Rugby Union grew from these rules. Other schools preferred the "hands free" game that relied on **dribbling** skills.

In 1848 the first general rules of the dribbling game, which became known as soccer, or football, were drawn up at Cambridge University. The Football Association was formed in 1863.

The name *soccer* developed from the letters *S*, *O*, and *C* in the word *Association,* but the game is known as *football* in most parts of the world.

FIFA

Soccer quickly gained popularity throughout Europe and South America. In 1904, seven nations—Belgium, Spain, Sweden, France, The Netherlands, Denmark, and Switzerland met in Paris to form FIFA, the Federation Internationale de Football Association. FIFA has been the governing body of world soccer ever since.

In 1900, soccer became the first team sport to be introduced to the Olympic Games. Since 1930, soccer has also been played every four years for the World Cup. This event attracts more television viewers than any other sporting event worldwide.

What You Need to Play

The field

Soccer is played on a rectangular field measuring between 100 to 130 yards (91 to 119 meters) long and 50 to 100 yards (46 to 91 meters) wide. Junior players play on fields approximately half this size.

There is a goal at each end of the field. The goals are in the center of the goal lines. They are 24 feet (7.32 meters) wide and 8 feet (2.44 meters) high. A net is strung across the back of the goal to catch the ball. The bar running across the top is called the crossbar.

Whose goal?

Each team defends their own goal. Players try to score by kicking or heading the ball into their opponents' goal.

Soccer is played on a grass field between two netted goals.

Shin guards are worn underneath socks to protect the shins from accidental kicks from other players.

The ball

The soccer ball is round and usually white. It is made from leather or a similar material. Balls are various sizes depending on the ages of the players:

Under nine years
    Size 3 (7 inch/18 centimeter diameter)
10-13 years
    Size 4 (8 inch/20 centimeter diameter)
14 years +
    Full size ball (8.5 inch/22 centimeter diameter).

Take care of your ball by keeping it filled with air. Do not play with it on asphalt or road surfaces because this may damage the ball. When you finish playing, wipe it so that it is clean and dry. Then store it in a dry place.

Clothing

For practice or for informal games at school, all you need are shorts, a T-shirt, socks, and soccer shoes that have cleats.

At a team or competitive level, each player on a team wears a uniform. The **goalkeeper** wears a different colored shirt than his or her teammates, and from their opponents. This is so that he

or she stands out from the other players. Goalkeepers wear gloves that are designed to protect the hands and wrists. They also help the goalkeeper grip the ball in wet weather.

Your footwear is your most important part of the uniform. Choose shoes that are comfortable—neither too tight nor too loose. Make sure they are well padded inside to prevent blisters.

Shin guards

Shin guards are required for matches to protect your ankles and shins. They are light and comfortable and do not restrict movement. Shin guards should also be worn during practice.

Rules

A referee controls the game. It is his or her job to begin the game, enforce the rules, decide whether a goal is legal, and end the game. A referee blows a whistle to signal the beginning or end of a game and to call a play.

Two **linesmen**, also known as assistant referees, patrol one **touchline** each. They assist the referee in calling plays.

Playing the ball

Players may strike the ball with any part of their body except their arms or hands. The only exception to this rule is the **goalkeeper,** who may catch and throw the ball when he or she is in the penalty area.

Start of play

To begin play, the two captains toss a coin to decide who will have choice of goal, and who will **kick off** first. Usually the winning captain chooses to kick off. The opposing captain then chooses which goal his or her team will defend. At half time, the kickoff goes to the other team. Play also begins with a kickoff after a goal is scored. The non-scoring team gets possession of the ball and kicks off.

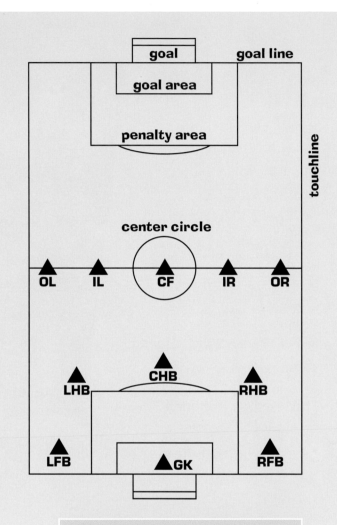

Field markings and player positions for the start of play.

GK goalkeeper
RFB right full back
LFB left full back
RHB right half back
CHB center half back
LHB left half back
OR outside right (winger)
IR inside right (striker)
CF center forward
IL inside left (striker)
OL outside left (winger)

The kickoff is taken on the halfway line inside the center circle. The ball must be kicked forward toward the opponent's goal.

At the kickoff, all members of the kicking team must be on the defensive half of the field—the half with their goal.

At the kick off, no member of the non-kicking team is allowed to be closer than 32 feet (10 meters) to the ball. They may only enter the center circle after the ball has been played.

Scoring goals

Players try to score by kicking or heading the ball into their opponent's goal. Any player can score a goal from any part of the field. A goal is scored when the ball passes completely over the goal line, between the two posts, and under the crossbar. It counts even if it touches any part of the goalposts or any player on its way in. If the ball rebounds from the crossbar or goalposts back onto the field, no goal is scored.

Ball in and out of play

The ball is out of play when the ball crosses over a boundary line, whether it is on the ground or in the air.

Whenever the ball crosses the touchline it is brought back into play by a **throw in**. The throw in is awarded to the opponents of the team that last touched the ball. A player from that team stands where the ball crossed the line. He or she stands with feet on, but not over the touchline, and throws the ball back into play.

When an **offensive** player puts the ball over his or her opponent's goal line, the ball is brought back into play by the goalkeeper with a **goal kick**. It is taken from the corner of the goal area. A teammate may only touch the ball once it has passed outside the penalty area.

When a **defending** player plays the ball over his or her own goal line, a **corner kick** is awarded to the other team. The ball is placed in the corner kick area and kicked back into play by a member of the attacking team.

A goal is scored when the ball passes over the goal line and into the net.

Rules

Fouls

Soccer rules do not allow you to jump at, push, trip, kick, hit, or interfere with an opponent. Nor may you touch the ball with your hands. These are fouls. They result in a **free kick** for the other team.

A **direct free kick** is awarded for a violent or serious foul. The player awarded the direct free kick may score a goal from it. For a less serious foul, an **indirect free kick** is awarded. The player awarded the indirect free kick must first pass the ball to a teammate before a goal can be scored. Opposition players must be at least 30 feet (9.15 meters) away when a player takes a free kick.

A **penalty kick** is awarded when a defending team fouls inside the penalty area. This is taken from the penalty spot which is 30 feet (9.15 meters) in front of the center of the goal. Only the **goalkeeper** and the player awarded the kick are allowed inside the penalty area until the ball is kicked. In some junior soccer games, a foul in the penalty area can result in a free kick being taken from the edge of the penalty area.

Handball

The only two players allowed to touch the ball with their hands or arms are the goalkeepers. If a field player handles the ball, his or her opponents receive a free kick. The offender may get a warning.

Player A passes the ball to teammate B. Player B is offside because there is only one defender (not the required two) between him and the goal line when the ball was played.

Offside

The **offside** rule is designed to keep an offensive player from waiting for the ball by the goal. If a teammate passes the ball to you, and there are fewer than two defenders between you and the goal line when the ball was played, then you are offside. You cannot be offside if you have possession of the ball.

The **linesman,** or referee's assistant, will raise his or her flag when a player is offside. An indirect free kick is awarded to the opponents.

Own goal

From time to time, a defender will head, deflect, or mistakenly kick the ball into his or her own goal. This counts as a legal goal for the other team. It is called an "own goal."

The referee's signals

Direct free kick
The referee's hand indicates which team is awarded the kick.

Indirect free kick
The referee holds his hand up.

Goal/penalty kick
The referee's hand points to the ground. Depending on where the hand points, either a goal kick or a penalty kick has been awarded.

Play on
The referee allows the team to play on even though he has seen an offense against them.

Official caution
The red card is shown after a warning yellow card. This happens when a player has repeatedly argued with the referee or deliberately broken a rule. If a player is shown the red card he or she is immediately sent off the field and banned from the next match.

Skills

To become a good soccer player, you will need to learn a wide range of skills. To **pass** and **dribble** the ball and to shoot for a goal, you must learn to control the ball. You will need to master the trap and the **throw in.** You must learn to tackle and **defend.** And you will need to learn special skills if you play **goalkeeper.**

Controlling the ball

To pass, dribble, or shoot the ball, you will first need to control it. You are allowed to use any part of your body other than your arms and hands to trap and control the ball. It is important to have good control of the ball before you kick it.

When the ball is coming in your direction:

- decide which part of your body will trap or control the ball
- get behind the line of the ball
- watch the ball closely at all times
- let your body cushion the ball as it strikes you
- keep your arms wide for balance.

Foot control

There are several ways to control the ball with your foot.

One is to trap the ball with the sole of your foot. As the ball nears, raise your foot with toes pointing upwards. Bring your foot down to trap the ball between your foot and the ground.

The other method of trapping the ball is with the side of the foot. Turn your foot sideways toward the oncoming ball. Let your foot "give" a little to cushion the ball so that it doesn't bounce away.

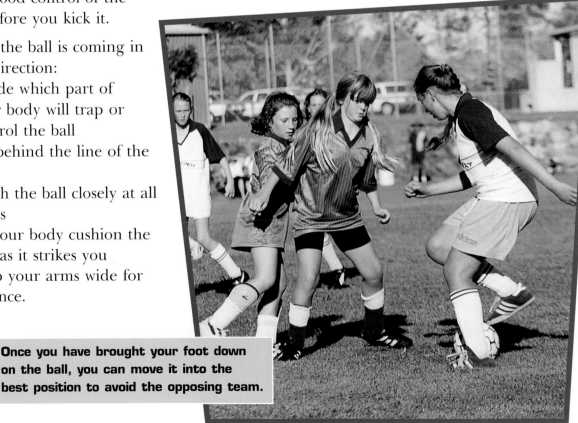

Once you have brought your foot down on the ball, you can move it into the best position to avoid the opposing team.

Chest control

Use your chest to trap and rebound the ball to the ground. Keep your arms away from your body for balance and to avoid a "handball" violation.

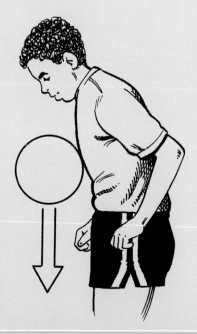

As the ball approaches, lean backwards, bend your knees, and relax your chest muscles.

Try to catch the ball on your chest. Keep your arms wide, and away from the ball to keep your balance. Move your upper body forward so that the ball drops to your feet.

Skills

Dribbling the ball

Dribbling is a very important soccer skill. It allows you to move yourself and the ball into position for **passing** or shooting, and to avoid tackles from your opponents. Push the ball along with your instep, or the side of your foot, as you run. The ball should always be within about three feet (one meter) of your feet. This will allow you to stop or to change directions quickly.

Start by moving slowly as you dribble. Concentrate on controlling the ball as you tap it along so that it doesn't move too far away. Watch the ball carefully until you have full control. As your skills improve, you will be able to look up to watch your opponents and teammates.

Always keep your balance and run only as quickly as you can and still change direction or speed comfortably. As your skills improve, practice confusing your opponents with rapid changes of speed and sudden stops.

Dribbling involves pushing the ball along with the side of your foot.

Passing the ball

Passing the ball accurately is a very important soccer skill. It allows you to advance the ball up the field and into a goal-scoring position. If your team's passing is not very accurate, your opponents will have better chances of getting possession of the ball.

There are different kinds of passes, but for each one it is important to follow these steps:

- Pass the ball to where your teammate is running, so that the player and the ball arrive in the same place at the same time.
- Pass the ball so that when it reaches your teammate it is on the ground. Your teammate will have an easier time controlling a rolling ball than a bouncing one.
- Always watch the ball closely and follow through toward your target.

Inside of the foot pass

The inside-of-the-foot pass is very accurate over short distances.

Approach the ball head on. Step with your non-kicking foot pointing toward your target and your knee slightly bent. Turn your kicking leg out, and with your foot parallel to the ground, kick the middle of the ball to keep it low. To raise the ball, strike it below its mid-point. Watch the ball as you make contact and follow through with your foot toward the target, keeping your knee high.

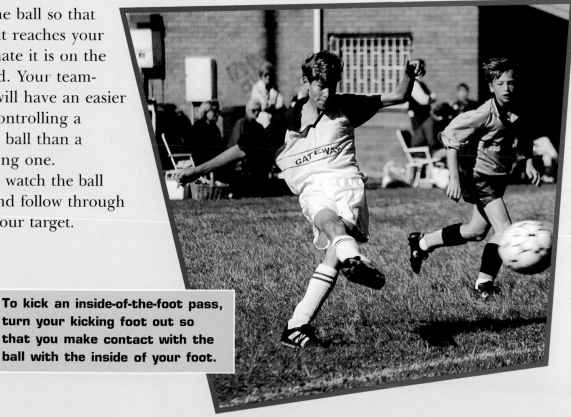

To kick an inside-of-the-foot pass, turn your kicking foot out so that you make contact with the ball with the inside of your foot.

Skills

Drive

The **drive** is the most powerful soccer kick. It allows you to **pass** long down the field or to shoot powerfully for a goal.

As you run behind the ball, take a long step and place your non-kicking foot a little behind the ball.

With your arms out wide to give you balance, kick the ball hard. Make contact with the ball with your instep. Kick under the ball to raise it. If you wish to keep the ball low, strike it in the middle. Keep your toes pointed down so that the laces make contact with the ball.

Drive

Keep your arms out wide for balance as you drive the ball.

Volley

Sometimes the ball will be bouncing or airborne as you receive it. You can either take the ball under control before you kick it or you can kick a **volley**. The volley involves kicking the ball while it is still in the air.

Move into the line of the ball and throw your arms out wide for balance. Bring your kicking knee up high. Keep your non-kicking leg slightly bent. Strike the middle or top of the ball to keep its flight low. Try to keep your kicking toe pointed down. Follow through in the direction of your target. You can use your shin to strike the ball if it is really high.

Volley

Watch the ball all the way onto your foot and follow through towards your target for a volley kick.

Toe kicks

In most cases, you should not kick the ball with your toes. A toe kick is usually inaccurate, and because the toe area of the shoe is usually very soft, it can be painful.

However, a toe kick may be useful in stealing a ball or poking at it. Toe kicks are also useful in crowded areas. Use it with caution.

Which direction?

The direction of your pass is determined by what part of the ball you strike and what part of your foot makes contact with the ball.

The ball will spin to the left when struck with the inside of the right foot.

The ball will swerve to the right when struck with the outside of the right foot.

Skills

Heading the ball

When the ball is airborne and above the height of your chest, you may **pass,** shoot, or knock the ball clear of the goal in **defense** by **heading** it. The power and control of the ball when heading comes from bending at the waist.

Keep your eyes on the ball as you position yourself to head it.

Move into position in the path of the ball with one foot in front of the other, leaning back slightly. Hold your hands wide apart and slightly forward.

Move forward powerfully from the waist. Keep your eyes on the ball and tense your neck muscles as you strike the ball from your forehead. Keep your upper body straight—don't bend your neck as you contact the ball. Follow through towards your target.

Use your forehead to head the ball. Your hairline, where your hair meets your forehead, is the ideal contact point. Avoid heading the ball from the top of your head because it can be quite painful.

Practice heading the ball from a stationary position until you have mastered the skill. Keep your eyes open and mouth closed.

Power heading

Power heading involves jumping up to head the ball. Judge quickly where you will meet the ball and move into position. Watch the ball very closely and meet it at the top of your jump. Hold your arms out for balance and draw your head back, ready to strike the ball. Bring your upper body forward and strike the ball forcefully with your forehead.

The throw in

When the ball goes out of play by crossing a **touchline,** it is brought back into play with a **throw in.** The throw in involves an overhead throw from the sideline.

Both of your feet must be on or behind the line as you throw the ball in one motion from behind and over your head. Both your feet must remain on the ground until the ball is released.

Skills

If you can shoot accurately and avoid the goalkeeper, you'll score for your team.

Shooting goals

Shooting goals is one of soccer's most exciting moments. Any player on the team may shoot for a goal from anywhere on the field. There are two important points that will help your team's chances of scoring a goal:

If you are close enough to shoot a goal, then shoot. But if a teammate is in a better position to shoot a goal, **pass** the ball to him or her.

Remember the saying, "Shoot low and in they go." Not only are low shots difficult for the **goalkeeper** to stop, but they often lead to another chance to score if they rebound off a post or the goalkeeper.

When you or one of your teammates has made a shot for goal, always be prepared for the ball to rebound. Don't take your eyes off the ball because you may be able to score off the rebounding ball.

Tackling and defending

Whenever your opponents have the ball, your team should tackle and try to win the ball back. Always stay close and guard your opponent. If your opponent gets the ball, move into a position where you are between him or her and the goal. By blocking the path, you will force him or her to pass or to try to move around you.

Challenging your opponent for the ball is known as a tackle.

Make contact with the ball when tackling, not with your opponent.

Block tackle

The block tackle is the most common and safest tackle. It usually takes place when you are in front of your opponent. Your opponent will try to dodge you, so try to move quickly to keep in front of him or her. Keep your eye on the ball.

Interception

If you can anticipate where a member of the opposing team will pass the ball, you can intercept it before it reaches an opposing player. Take control as quickly as you can and **dribble** or pass the ball to a teammate.

Block tackle

Get into position facing your opponent. As he or she approaches, slowly move backwards.

As your opponent moves farther forward, move your body forward and bring your leg into contact with the ball.

Your opponent will need to lift his or her leg to avoid tripping and you can push the ball forward to gain possession.

Skills

Goalkeeping

Goalkeeping is a specialist position. It calls for skills that are entirely different from those required of the 10 other players. A goalkeeper needs to be courageous and quick. He or she must be able to bend, spring, and jump quickly in any direction to keep a ball from going into the goal.

The goalkeeper should try to keep his or her body in line with the ball at all times. Only dive for the ball when you have no other choice.

For a high ball, jump up and catch the ball, bringing it quickly down to your chest as you land.

For a low ball, kneel on one knee in the path of the ball and scoop it up into your chest with your hands.

Diving

When diving to save a wide ball, move quickly by extending your body sideways. Stretch one arm to get your hand behind the ball. If possible, bring your other hand up to grab it. Try to cushion your fall as you land, but be careful not to release the ball.

Having saved the attempt at goal, you should move quickly to throw, kick, or roll the ball to a teammate. A roll or a throw is very accurate and is often the best choice.

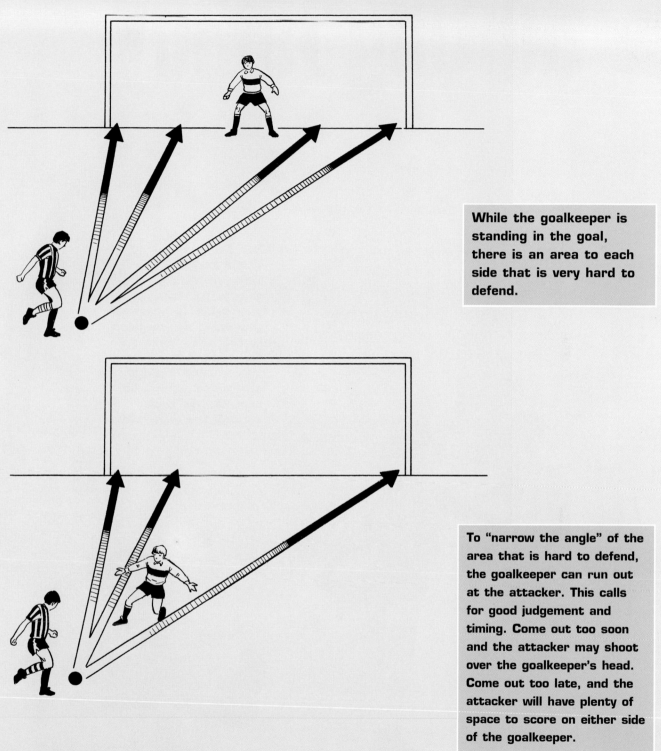

While the goalkeeper is standing in the goal, there is an area to each side that is very hard to defend.

To "narrow the angle" of the area that is hard to defend, the goalkeeper can run out at the attacker. This calls for good judgement and timing. Come out too soon and the attacker may shoot over the goalkeeper's head. Come out too late, and the attacker will have plenty of space to score on either side of the goalkeeper.

Narrowing the angle

The goalkeeper may come forward out of the goal area to defend the goal. If he or she comes forward, the angle being defended will be smaller. If the attacking player shoots, the goalkeeper will have a good chance of intercepting the ball.

But if the attacking player dodges around the goalkeeper or **passes** to another player, the goalkeeper may not be able to keep the ball out of the goal.

Getting Ready

Before you begin practice or a game, it is important that your body is warm. Soccer requires you to use most muscle groups in your body, especially the leg, trunk, and neck muscles. Start by doing the following stretches and exercises. Repeat each one four to six times times. Then jog or skip rope for about five minutes.

Side Bends
Stand upright with one hand on your waist. Bring your other arm up over your head as you bend to the side. Make sure you don't lean forward as you bend. Hold the stretch for about 15 seconds and then stretch the other side.

Quadriceps Stretch
Hold a partner with one hand for balance. Bend one knee and gently pull your foot up behind you. Hold the stretch for about 15 seconds and then stretch the other leg.

Hamstring and Lower Back Stretch
Sit on the floor with one leg stretched out straight in front. Reach forward to the toes of your straight leg, keeping your back as straight as possible. Hold the stretch for about 15 seconds and then change legs.

Push Ups
Lie on the ground, face down, with your toes tucked under and your hands beside your shoulders. Push up with your arms, keeping your body straight. Then lower your body to the floor.

Neck Stretch
Gently pull your head towards your shoulder until you feel the stretch. Hold for about 15 seconds and then stretch the other side.

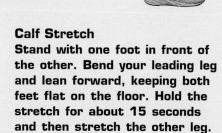

Lower Back Stretch
Lie on your back with your legs outstretched. Bend one knee up to your chest and lift your head and shoulders off the floor to meet it. Lower yourself and then stretch the other side.

Calf Stretch
Stand with one foot in front of the other. Bend your leading leg and lean forward, keeping both feet flat on the floor. Hold the stretch for about 15 seconds and then stretch the other leg.

Treadmills
Put your hands on the ground, shoulder-width apart, and have your legs stretched behind you. Bring one foot forward. Replace it and then bring the other foot up.

Taking it Further

The U.S. Soccer Federation
1811 South Prairie Avenue
Chicago, IL
☎ (312) 808-1300

The U.S. Youth Soccer Association
2050 North Plano Road
Richardson, TX 75082
☎ (800) 4-SOCCER

American Youth Soccer Organization
5403 West 138th Street
Hawthorne, CA 90250
☎ (800) 872- 2976

Women's Soccer Foundation
PO Box 2097
Norton, MA 02766-0993
☎ (508) 285-5699

More Books to Read

Coleman, Lori. *Fundamental Soccer.* Minneapolis, Minn: Lerner Publishing Group, 1995.

Stewart, Mark. *Soccer: An Intimate History of the World's Most Popular Game.* Danbury, Conn: Franklin Watts Incorporated, 1998.

Wilner, Barry. *Soccer.* Austin, Tex: Raintree Steck-Vaughn Publishers, 1995.

Glossary

corner kick free kick taken from a corner of the field by the attacking team after the defending team has kicked the ball over their goal line

defense team without the ball, trying to stop their opponents from scoring

direct free kick free kick given to a team because of a serious foul; a goal may be scored from a direct free kick without another player touching the ball

dribble moving the ball with the feet

drive strong kick of the ball that goes a long distance

free kick kick awarded after a foul

goalkeeper player who is positioned directly in front of his or her goal; the only player on each team allowed to use his or her hands

goal kick kick awarded to the **goalkeeper** of the defending team when the ball is sent over the goal line by the attacking team

heading using the forehead to strike the ball

indirect free kick free kick given to a team because of a foul; a goal may only be scored after another player from either team has touched the ball

kick off when the ball is kicked from the center of the field to start the game or to restart it at half time and after a goal is scored

linesmen assistant referees who signal to the referee with a raised flag when an illegal play is made

offense team with the ball trying to score a goal

offside foul called when an attacking player without the ball does not have two defenders between himself or herself and the goal

pass transfer of the ball from one player to another

penalty kick free kick awarded to the attacking team when a defender commits a serious foul in the penalty area; only the goalkeeper can defend the penalty kick

shin guards protective pads for the shins and ankles.

striker forward player whose most important job is to score goals

throw in when the ball crosses a touchline and goes out, play is restarted with a throw in from the **touchline**

touchlines side boundary lines of the soccer field

volley to kick the ball while it is in the air

wingers attacking players whose position is out wide on the field

Index